Gran-Gran's Best Trick

BY

DWIGHT HOLDEN, M.D.

ILLUSTRATED BY

MICHAEL CHESWORTH

MAGINATION PRESS
NEW YORK

Library of Congress Cataloging-in-Publication Data

Holden, L. Dwight.
   Gran-gran's best trick : a story for children who have lost
someone they love / written by L. Dwight Holden ; illustrated by
   Michael Chesworth.
      p.   cm.
   Summary: A child recounts his special relationships with his
grandfather and the difficulty of coping with his death from cancer.
   ISBN 0-945354-16-9
   1. Bereavement in children—Juvenile literature.   2. Children and
death—Juvenile literature.   3. Grandparents—Death—Psychological
aspects—Juvenile literature.   4. Terminally ill—Family
relationships—Juvenile literature.   5. Cancer—Patients—Family
relationships—Juvenile literature.   [1. Death. 2. Cancer—
Patients. 3. Terminally ill. 4. Grandfathers.]   I. Chesworth,
Michael, ill.   II. Title.
BF723.G75H65   1989
155.9'37—dc20
                                                    89-8336
                                                       CIP
                                                        AC

Copyright © 1989 by L. Dwight Holden
Published by
Magination Press
An Imprint of Brunner/Mazel, Inc., 19 Union Square West, New York, NY 10003
Paperback edition distributed to the trade by
Publishers Group West
4065 Hollis St., Emeryville, CA 94608
Telephone 800-365-3453; in CA call collect 415-658-3453
Distributed in Canada by
Book Center
1140 Beaulac St., Montreal, Quebec H4R 1R8, Canada

MANUFACTURED IN THE UNITED STATES OF AMERICA

10 9 8 7 6 5 4 3 2 1

Introduction for Parents

The death of someone we love is one of the most difficult and painful experiences of life for us all. For children it is equally painful, but even harder to grasp. As parents we want desperately to protect our children from that pain, but we cannot. What we can do is help them get through it.

Children cannot be shielded from loss because it is their experience, too. They see it, hear it, and feel the pain. Whether or not they ask questions, the questions are there. Why does he have to be sick? Why does she have to die? Why do I hurt so much? Helping your children struggle with these and other questions lets them know you trust them to be able to handle their feelings. This builds a stronger, more secure sense of self, which is one of the gains that can grow from the loss.

This story was written to help children deal with the loss of someone they love, and to help you help your children with that loss. It is a true story about one young girl's experience with her grandfather's illness and death by cancer and her struggle to gain something from the loss. The lessons she learned can also apply to other situations and other forms of loss, such as from divorce or moving away.

The book is designed for elementary school age children. It may be read either by the child or by the parent to the child. Either way, it may be best to read it the first time together. Be prepared to answer questions honestly. Or your child may ponder it for a while and ask later. And hopefully some of your child's questions will be answered by the book itself.

While this book is about death and about loss, it is about more than that. It is about how we, whether children or adults, can learn and grow from the experience. It is also about how those we love never leave our hearts. That is love's best trick.

For Gran-Gran
Who Taught Without Teaching

Gran-Gran has cancer.
I don't really know what that means,
but it must be something terrible.
Something about this stuff growing
inside of him that shouldn't be there
and it's growing bigger and they can't
stop it. I don't know why they can't
stop it, but they can't. All I know is
Gran-Gran is sick.

He just lies there. He doesn't do
anything anymore.
     No fishing.
     No gardening.
     No fixing things in the garage.

Sometimes when I come to see
Gran-Gran and Nana, he doesn't even
smile. (Gran-Gran always smiles.)
And he doesn't listen to me.
He just lies there.

That's not my Gran-Gran; I'm sure of
it. My Gran-Gran listens to me.
    He smiles at me.
    He hugs me.
    He tickles me.
    He lets me ride piggy-back.
    He takes me fishing and baits
        my hook for me.
    He takes me on long safaris
        through the neighborhood
        or out by the lake.

Gran-Gran used to take me on lots of
safaris. We didn't hunt for a lion or a
rhinoceros, just stuff. . .
special stuff.

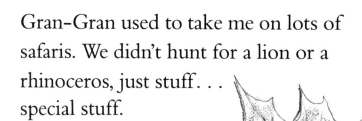

Giant leaves,

tiny mushrooms with
little red caps,

dandelions (we always
blew the fuzz away),
and rocks.

Gran-Gran and I loved rocks. Little ones, crooked or smooth, shiny or plain, colored or brown. Sometimes he found stuff I didn't notice. "Oh, just looky here!" he would say. He always saw what everyone else walked past, and suddenly it became

SOMETHING.

I always had this warm feeling inside
just walking along

holding his hand,

listening to him whistle,

trying to whistle too,

and looking
for treasures.

When the safari was over, he would lie down right in the middle of the living room.

He put a newspaper over his face and took a catnap, no matter how noisy it was. But, sometimes I would peek under the paper and he would grab me and shout, "BOO!"

I would scream.
Then I would laugh.
With Gran–Gran, even being scared felt safe.

When Elizabeth was born, all she did
was cry, eat, sleep, and poop in her
diapers, but everyone thought she
was wonderful and brought her gobs
of presents.

I got a pat on the head
(if I was lucky).

I thought
I had become
invisible.

But not with Gran-Gran.
I always knew he
still saw me, too,
like that extra special
treasure rock on our safari.
I wish we could go on
safaris like we used to.
Now he can barely get out
of bed.

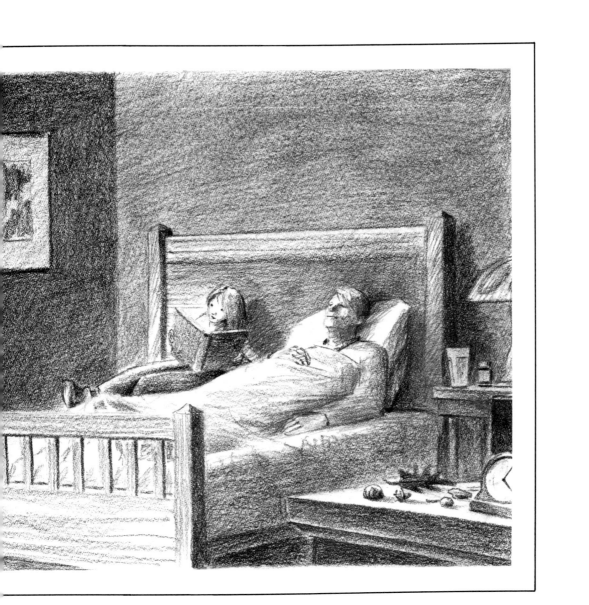

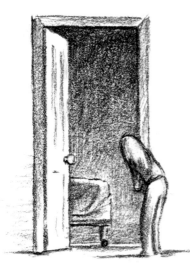

Gran-Gran seems like a stranger now. He acts different. He just lies in bed. Sometimes he sleeps. Sometimes he just looks off at nothing, as if he sees a TV that nobody else sees. And he groans. Every time he moves, he groans. Except when he knows I'm watching; then he grits his teeth. It's awful, but everyone acts like I shouldn't be upset.

I'm upset.

It's horrible. Gran-Gran's skinny. Except his face—it's all puffy. (If something is growing inside of him, why is he getting so thin?) He's really pale, and all his hair fell out, except for a few little grey curly ones. Mom and Dad say it's the medicine the doctors gave him to kill the cancer. Something about it eating the cancer, which is good, but also eating part of him, which is bad. Stupid medicine! Why can't it tell the difference between the cancer and my Gran-Gran?

Gran-Gran is in the hospital again.
He keeps going in and out. There
are all these tubes and bottles and
bags hooked to him. I always thought
that if medicine was awful, at least it
made me well. But Gran-Gran isn't
getting well.

I don't want to be here.

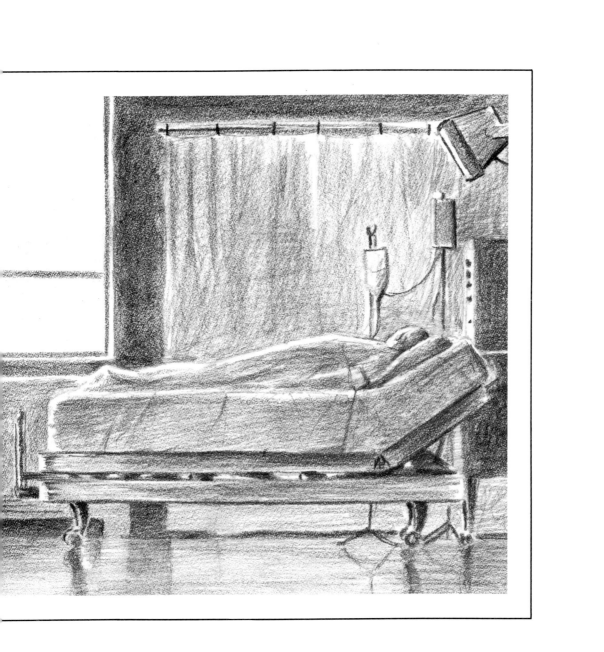

He doesn't know me.

He doesn't see me.

He sees fish.

He throws his arm out like he's
got his fishing rod,
and then he reels the fish in.

But there's no fish and no lake in his hospital room.

Mom and Dad asked if I had any
questions.

I said no.

I have lots of questions, but
I don't think I will like the
answers.

I want my old
Gran-Gran back.

Gran-Gran
died
today.

My Dad just told me. I can't believe
it, but that's what he said.

I really don't understand at all. He
died because the cancer was growing,
but now I guess the cancer died too.
Why couldn't the cancer just die and
leave Gran-Gran with us?

Dad held me close and said it was okay to cry. Then we both cried, and then we stopped, and then we cried again.

It wasn't okay.

I want my
Gran-Gran
back.

I went to Gran-Gran's funeral. Mom and Dad said I didn't have to go. I said I didn't want to, but then I did. I had to see.

There were lots of people there. They sang songs and prayed and talked about him.

Nana cried.
Mom and Dad cried.
My cousins and
aunts and
uncles cried.
I cried.

And there was Gran-Gran
lying in this thing they call
a casket. I was so scared.
It looked like Gran-Gran
again, not like that stranger.
He didn't look sick anymore.
How did they do that?

Except Gran-Gran
didn't wear suits
that much. He wore
fishing clothes.

But he looked so pale and his eyes
were shut. I kept waiting for them
to open. Maybe he was just taking
a catnap. But his eyes didn't open.
Then I touched him. Maybe he
would wake up. But his skin was

so cold and he felt hard, like wax.
I started to shiver all over.

Then they put the top down on the
casket and closed him up in there. . .
all alone.

Everyone cried again.

Gran-Gran is dead. I don't even know
what that means. All I know is he's
gone and I can't find him. When we
go to Nana and Gran-Gran's house
it's so quiet. I walk into the room and
expect to find him in his special easy
chair watching TV and shelling
pecans and smiling and reaching
out to hug me.

But he's not there.

Then I look out back in the garage to see if he's fixing something or working on his fishing boat, just like he always did. Gran-Gran could fix anything.
But the garage is locked up tight.

It used to be when I would fall out of the swing and scrape my knees, I would start to cry. Gran-Gran would say, "Hey, that was a good trick! Can I see that one again?" Then I would laugh and it didn't hurt so much.
Now that was a good trick!

But this one still hurts. Gran-Gran's done a trick, and I don't like this one. He's gone and I didn't say he could go. I don't know where he went. Mom and Dad say he's gone to heaven and we'll see him again someday. But I want to see him now.

Gran-Gran isn't here anymore, so I'll have to remember him. Once, I gave him a book about grandparents to write in so he could tell me about himself. (Gran-Gran never talked much about himself.) After he died, Nana gave it back to me.

On one page it said, "I collect . . .
grandkids and ice coolers." He always
collected plastic ice coolers to plant
seeds for his garden. The backyard
was full of old coolers with plants in
them. It looked messy, but Gran-
Gran didn't care. When I see coolers,
I think of him.

I will remember Gran-Gran,
but not bent over and pale.

I will remember him with his
fishing hat and pole.

I will remember the funny
little cackle in his laugh.

I will remember he made
the best tacos in the
whole world.

Elizabeth is too little to remember him
so I will have to tell her all about him.

About ice cooler gardens.

About fishing.

About piggy-back rides.

About safaris.

Especially about safaris.

I'll teach her how to see things like
he did that nobody else noticed. Then
she will know Gran-Gran like I do,
even though he's gone.

Maybe that's Gran-Gran's
best trick ever.

Other Magination Press Books include:

Cartoon Magic: How to Help Children Discover Their Rainbows Within
by Richard J. Crowley, Ph.D., and Joyce C. Mills, Ph.D.

Clouds and Clocks: A Story for Children Who Soil
by Matthew Galvin, M.D.

Gran-Gran's Best Trick: A Story for Children Who Have Lost Someone They Love
by L. Dwight Holden, M.D.

Ignatius Finds Help: A Story About Psychotherapy for Children
by Matthew Galvin, M.D.

Lizard Tales: Observations About Life
by William R. Davis, M.D.

Otto Learns About His Medicine: A Story About Medication for Hyperactive Children
by Matthew Galvin, M.D.

Robby Really Transforms: A Story About Grown-ups Helping Children
by Matthew Galvin, M.D.

Sammy the Elephant and Mr. Camel: A Story to Help Children Overcome Bedwetting While Discovering Self-Appreciation
by Joyce C. Mills, Ph.D., and Richard J. Crowley, Ph.D.

This Is Me and My Single Parent: A Discovery Workbook for Children and Single Parents
by Marla D. Evans

This Is Me and My Two Families: An Awareness Scrapbook/Journal for Children Living in Stepfamilies
by Marla D. Evans